FILM LISTOGRAPHY
YOUR LIFE IN MOVIE LISTS

CREATED BY   LISA   NOLA
ILLUSTRATIONS BY JON   STICH

CHRONICLE BOOKS
SAN FRANCISCO

ISBN 978-1-4521-0651-9

MANUFACTURED IN CHINA
DESIGN BY SUZANNE LAGASA
ILLUSTRATIONS AND HAND LETTERING BY JON STICH

CHRONICLE BOOKS PUBLISHES DISTINCTIVE BOOKS AND GIFTS. FROM
AWARD-WINNING CHILDREN'S TITLES, BEST-SELLING COOKBOOKS, AND ECLECTIC
POP CULTURE TO ACCLAIMED WORKS OF ART AND DESIGN, STATIONERY,
AND JOURNALS, WE CRAFT PUBLISHING THAT'S INSTANTLY RECOGNIZABLE
FOR ITS SPIRIT AND CREATIVITY. ENJOY OUR PUBLISHING AND BECOME
PART OF OUR COMMUNITY AT WWW.CHRONICLEBOOKS.COM.

10 9 8 7 6 5 4 3 2

CHRONICLE BOOKS LLC
680 SECOND STREET
SAN FRANCISCO, CA 94107
WWW.CHRONICLEBOOKS.COM

THIS BOOK IS DEDICATED TO MY LONGTIME LEADING MAN:
ADAM MARKS

"A FILM IS—OR SHOULD BE— MORE LIKE MUSIC THAN LIKE FICTION. IT SHOULD BE A PROGRESSION OF MOODS AND FEELINGS. THE THEME, WHAT'S BEHIND THE EMOTION, THE MEANING, ALL THAT COMES LATER." —STANLEY KUBRICK

FILM IS A POWERFUL MEDIUM THAT BROADENS OUR EXPERIENCE AND UNDERSTANDING OF THE WORLD AND OF EACH OTHER. FILM CAN ALLOW US TO ESCAPE FROM OUR LIVES OR CAN INSPIRE THEM. EVERY TUESDAY, MY DAD TOOK ME TO THE TWO-DOLLAR MOVIE THEATER, AND I GREW UP TO BE AN ARDENT MOVIE LOVER. MANY MOVIES IN MY OWN LISTOGRAPHY CONNECT WITH A SPECIFIC TIME IN MY LIFE AND HAD A TREMENDOUS INFLUENCE ON WHO I AM TODAY. **FILM LISTOGRAPHY** IS MY THANK-YOU TO ALL THE PEOPLE WHO MAKE GREAT FILMS, AND IT'S A VALUABLE REFERENCE WHEN I WANT TO RETURN TO A PARTICULAR ROMANCE OR ADVENTURE, OR WHEN I WANT A GOOD LAUGH OR CRY. I HOPE YOU ENJOY CONJURING UP YOUR FILM MEMORIES. OUR FAVORITES OFTEN SAY A LOT ABOUT WHO WE WERE, ARE, AND HOPE TO BE.

LISA NOLA
WWW.LISTOGRAPHY.COM

HAROLD AND MAUDE

LIST YOUR FAVORITE FILMS OF ALL TIME

LOST IN TRANSLATION

LIST INDEPENDENT FILMS YOU LOVE

HOWARD THE DUCK

LIST MOVIES YOU WALKED OUT ON

AMÉLIE

LIST YOUR TOP FOREIGN FILMS

LA JETÉE

LIST UNIQUE ART HOUSE FILMS YOU'VE SEEN

STONEHENGE STAGE PROP DEBACLE IN
THIS IS SPINAL TAP

LIST YOUR FAVORITE COMEDIES AND THEIR FUNNIEST MOMENT

THE SHINING

LIST HORROR FILMS THAT FREAK YOU OUT

THE KING OF KONG: A
FISTFUL OF QUARTERS

LIST YOUR TOP PICKS FOR DOCUMENTARIES

WALL·E

LIST YOUR FAVORITE ANIMATED FILMS

TRINITY'S OPENING FIGHT SCENE IN
THE MATRIX

LIST SPECIAL EFFECTS THAT BLEW YOUR MIND

THE KARATE KID
"WAX ON, WAX OFF. WAX ON, WAX OFF."

LIST FILMS THAT HAD A BIG INFLUENCE ON YOU

THE TRAMP GETS HIS GIRL IN CHARLIE CHAPLIN'S
CITY LIGHTS

LIST THE MOST ROMANTIC MOMENTS IN FILM

THE WIZARD OF OZ

LIST YOUR FAVORITE MOVIES FROM THE GOLDEN AGE
OF HOLLYWOOD (1920s TO THE 1950s)

EASY RIDER, DIRECTED BY DENNIS HOPPER

LIST YOUR FAVORITE FILMS FROM THE '60s

THE WARRIORS, DIRECTED BY WALTER HILL

LIST YOUR FAVORITE FILMS FROM THE '70s

PRETTY IN PINK, SCREENPLAY BY JOHN HUGHES

LIST YOUR FAVORITE FILMS FROM THE '80s

GLENGARRY GLEN ROSS,
SCREENPLAY BY DAVID MAMET

LIST YOUR FAVORITE FILMS FROM THE '90s

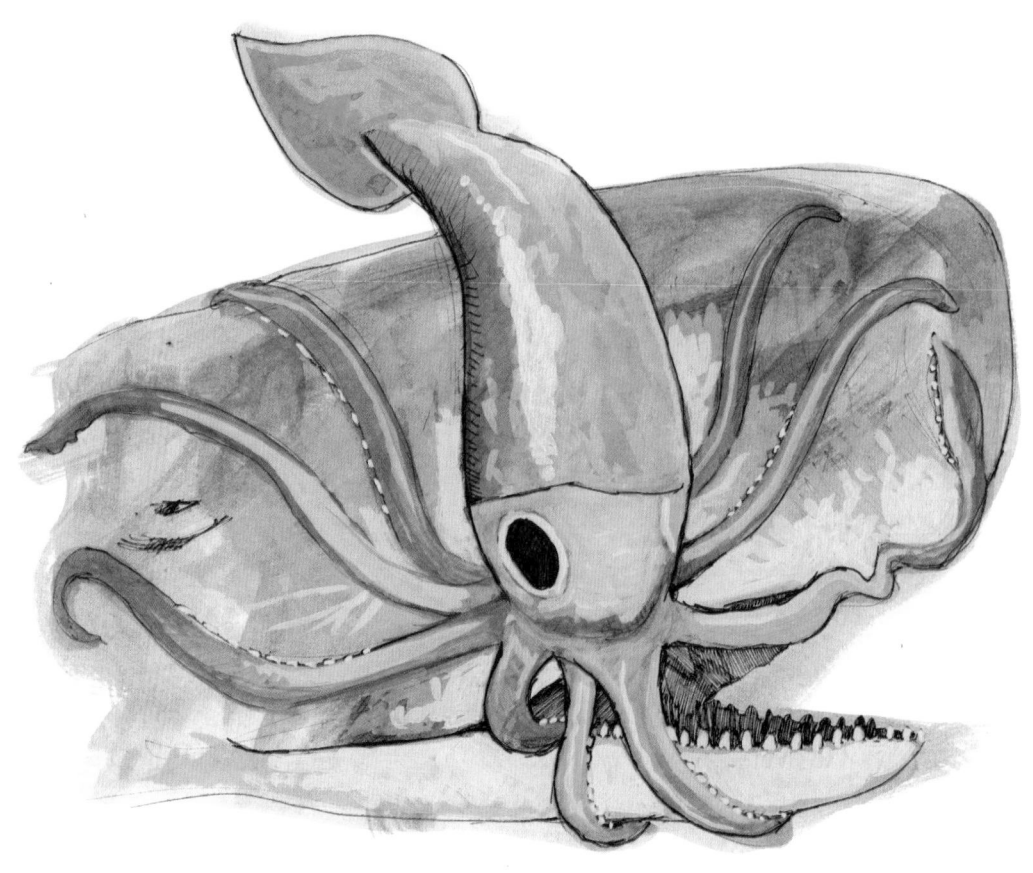

THE SQUID AND THE WHALE
DIRECTED BY NOAH BAUMBACH

LIST YOUR FAVORITE FILMS FROM THE '00s

THE MUPPETS TAKE MANHATTAN

LIST MOVIES YOU WATCHED GROWING UP THAT ALL KIDS SHOULD SEE

BUCK SWOPE OF **BOOGIE NIGHTS**

LIST CELLULOID CHARACTERS YOU WISH WERE YOUR FRIENDS

SEX AND THE CITY: THE MOVIE

"ON YOUR LEFT, CARRIE BRADSHAW'S APARTMENT."

LIST YOUR MOST EMBARRASSING
GUILTY-PLEASURE MOVIES

THE DARK KNIGHT

LIST COMIC BOOK ADAPTATIONS
YOU GIVE A THUMBS-UP

TRAINSPOTTING

LIST YOUR FAVORITE FILMS ADAPTED FROM BOOKS

BREAKFAST AT TIFFANY'S

LIST CLASSIC FILMS YOU'D LOVE TO SEE REMADE

HEDWIG AND THE ANGRY INCH

LIST MUSICALS OR MUSIC-RELATED FILMS YOU WANT IN YOUR ULTIMATE COLLECTION

"I WOULD NEVER WANT TO BELONG TO ANY CLUB THAT WOULD HAVE SOMEONE LIKE ME FOR A MEMBER."
—ALVY SINGER, ANNIE HALL

LIST FILM QUOTES YOU'LL NEVER FORGET

THE DIVING BELL AND THE BUTTERFLY

LIST FILMS THAT MAKE YOU CRY

FROGS RAINING FROM THE SKY IN
MAGNOLIA

LIST THE BEST MOVIE MOMENTS
OF ALL TIME

GEORGE LUCAS'S DARTH VADER

LIST VILLAINS YOU LOVE TO HATE

LASSIE

LIST MOVIE HEROES THAT WOULD MAKE YOUR DREAM TEAM

REQUIEM FOR A DREAM
BROOKLYN ROOFTOP, SUMMER 2007

LIST YOUR GREAT
MOVIE-WATCHING EXPERIENCES

TWIN PEAKS : FIRE WALK WITH ME,
SCORED BY ANGELO BADALAMENTI

LIST SOUNDTRACKS AND SCORES YOU LOVE

Campion
Bergman
Almodóvar
  Scorsese
  Moore
  Godard
    Gilliam
The   Weinsteins

LIST YOUR FAVORITE DIRECTORS AND PRODUCERS

DANIEL DAY-LEWIS

LIST YOUR FAVORITE ACTORS

DREW BARRYMORE

LIST YOUR FAVORITE ACTRESSES

SYLVESTER STALLONE

LIST MOVIE STARS
YOU CAN'T BEAR TO WATCH

CHARLIE KAUFMAN

LIST SCREENWRITERS
THAT NEVER LET YOU DOWN

MALCOLM X

LIST YOUR FAVORITE FILMS
ABOUT SOCIAL CHANGE

MARILYN MONROE'S DEATH

LIST MEMORABLE MOVIE-STAR NEWS STORIES

THE MICHAEL HUTCHENCE STORY

LIST SUBJECTS YOU'D LIKE TO SEE MADE INTO A FILM

AMERICAN SPLENDOR
HARVEY PEKAR

LIST THE BIOPICS YOU LOVE

APOCALYPSE NOW

LIST YOUR FAVORITE HISTORICAL DRAMAS

THE USUAL SUSPECTS

LIST YOUR FAVORITE MYSTERY AND SUSPENSE FILMS

"THAT'S THE DAY I REALIZED THAT THERE WAS THIS ENTIRE LIFE BEHIND THINGS, AND THIS INCREDIBLY BENEVOLENT FORCE THAT WANTED ME TO KNOW THERE WAS NO REASON TO BE AFRAID. EVER."

RICKY FITTS'S MONOLOGUE IN
AMERICAN BEAUTY

LIST MONOLOGUES THAT LEFT AN INDELIBLE MARK ON YOU

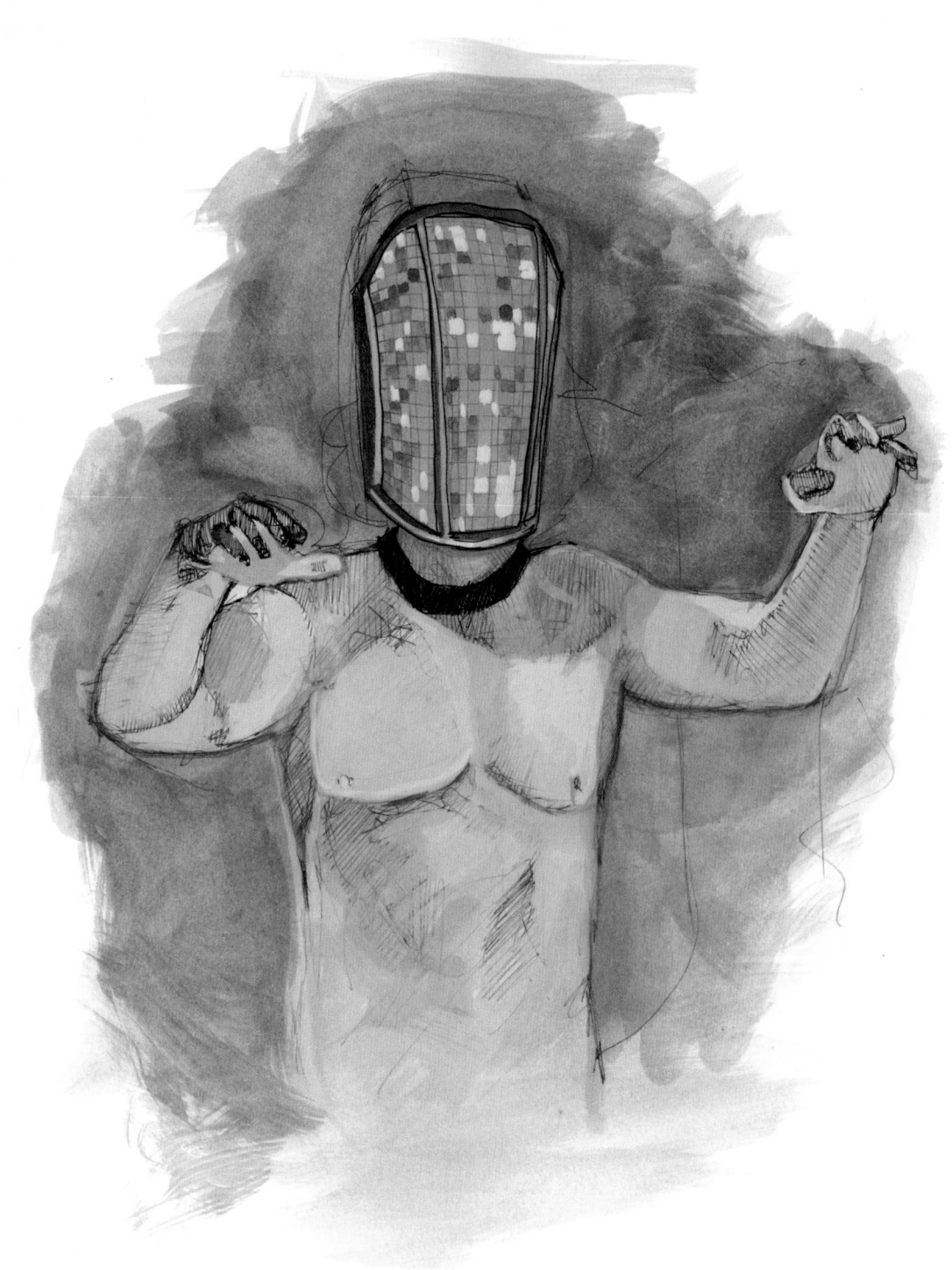

THE ANDROMEDA STRAIN, 1971

LIST YOUR TOP SCIENCE FICTION PICKS

MUMBAI IN
SLUMDOG MILLIONAIRE

LIST FILMS THAT CAPTURE
A PARTICULAR CITY OR PLACE PERFECTLY

his open face as the clearing light
of the sun shines in his eyes.
it is a face of peace, love, a face
of true, deep serenity.

CHRISTOPHER McCANDLESS'S DEATH IN
INTO THE WILD, DIRECTED BY SEAN PENN

LIST UNFORGETTABLE DEATH SCENES

MARK WAHLBERG

LIST YOUR BIGGEST HOLLYWOOD SAME-SEX CRUSHES

ROBERT PATTINSON
OR TAYLOR LAUTNER—
I CAN'T DECIDE!

LIST STARS YOU'D LIKE TO DATE

THELMA AND LOUISE

LIST FILM DUOS YOU LOVE

FAST TIMES AT
RIDGEMONT HIGH

LIST THE BEST PARTY MOVIES

PLAN 9 FROM OUTER SPACE
SO BAD, BUT SO GOOD

LIST YOUR TOP SO-BAD-IT'S-GOOD MOVIES

CLEMENTINE KRUCZYNSKI IN
ETERNAL SUNSHINE OF THE
SPOTLESS MIND

LIST CHARACTERS YOU ARE MOST LIKE

THE ROYAL TENENBAUMS

LIST MOVIE FAMILIES YOU'D HAPPILY JOIN

THE LORD OF THE RINGS

LIST YOUR FAVORITE ADVENTURE FILMS

VINCENT ACCIDENTALLY SHOOTS
MARVIN IN QUENTIN TARANTINO'S
PULP FICTION

LIST MOVIE SCENES THAT MADE YOU CRINGE

GREASE

LIST MOVIES THAT HAD THE BEST COSTUMES

THE BIG LEBOWSKI
MY DAD THINKS HE'S "THE DUDE"

LIST FILM CHARACTERS THAT REMIND YOU OF PEOPLE YOU KNOW

BOYZ N THE HOOD

LIST YOUR FAVORITE GANGSTER MOVIES

KIWI!

LIST YOUR FAVORITE SHORT FILMS

PAN'S LABYRINTH

LIST THE BEST FANTASY FILMS

MY FAVORITE CURSE WORD IS "CRUD"

LIST YOUR ANSWERS TO PIVOT'S / LIPTON'S INSIDE THE ACTORS STUDIO QUESTIONS

CONCERT SCENE IN
THE DOORS

LIST MOVIE MOMENTS YOU WISH YOU WERE AN EXTRA IN

ISAAC ASIMOV'S FOUNDATION SERIES

LIST BOOKS YOU'D LIKE TO SEE ADAPTED TO FILM

THE ROCKY HORROR PICTURE SHOW

LIST THE CULT FILMS YOU'LL ALWAYS LOVE

--- --- --- --- --- --- --- --- --- --- --- --- --- --- ---

--- --- --- --- --- --- --- --- --- --- --- --- --- --- ---

--- --- --- --- --- --- --- --- --- --- --- --- --- --- ---

--- --- --- --- --- --- --- --- --- --- --- --- --- --- ---

--- --- --- --- --- --- --- --- --- --- --- --- --- --- ---

--- --- --- --- --- --- --- --- --- --- --- --- --- --- ---

--- --- --- --- --- --- --- --- --- --- --- --- --- --- ---

--- --- --- --- --- --- --- --- --- --- --- --- --- --- ---

--- --- --- --- --- --- --- --- --- --- --- --- --- --- ---

--- --- --- --- --- --- --- --- --- --- --- --- --- --- ---

--- --- --- --- --- --- --- --- --- --- --- --- --- --- ---

--- --- --- --- --- --- --- --- --- --- --- --- --- --- ---

--- --- --- --- --- --- --- --- --- --- --- --- --- --- ---

--- --- --- --- --- --- --- --- --- --- --- --- --- --- ---

--- --- --- --- --- --- --- --- --- --- --- --- --- --- ---

--- --- --- --- --- --- --- --- --- --- --- --- --- --- ---

--- --- --- --- --- --- --- --- --- --- --- --- --- --- ---

OMAHA BEACH, D-DAY,
IN SAVING PRIVATE RYAN

LIST AMAZING ACTION SCENES

MOULIN ROUGE!

LIST THE MOVIE SETS YOU'D WANT TO LIVE ON

"ARTHUR'S THEME"

LIST MOVIE THEME SONGS YOU'D PUT ON YOUR PLAYLIST

MAD MEN

LIST TV SHOWS YOU WANT TO SEE TURNED INTO MOVIES

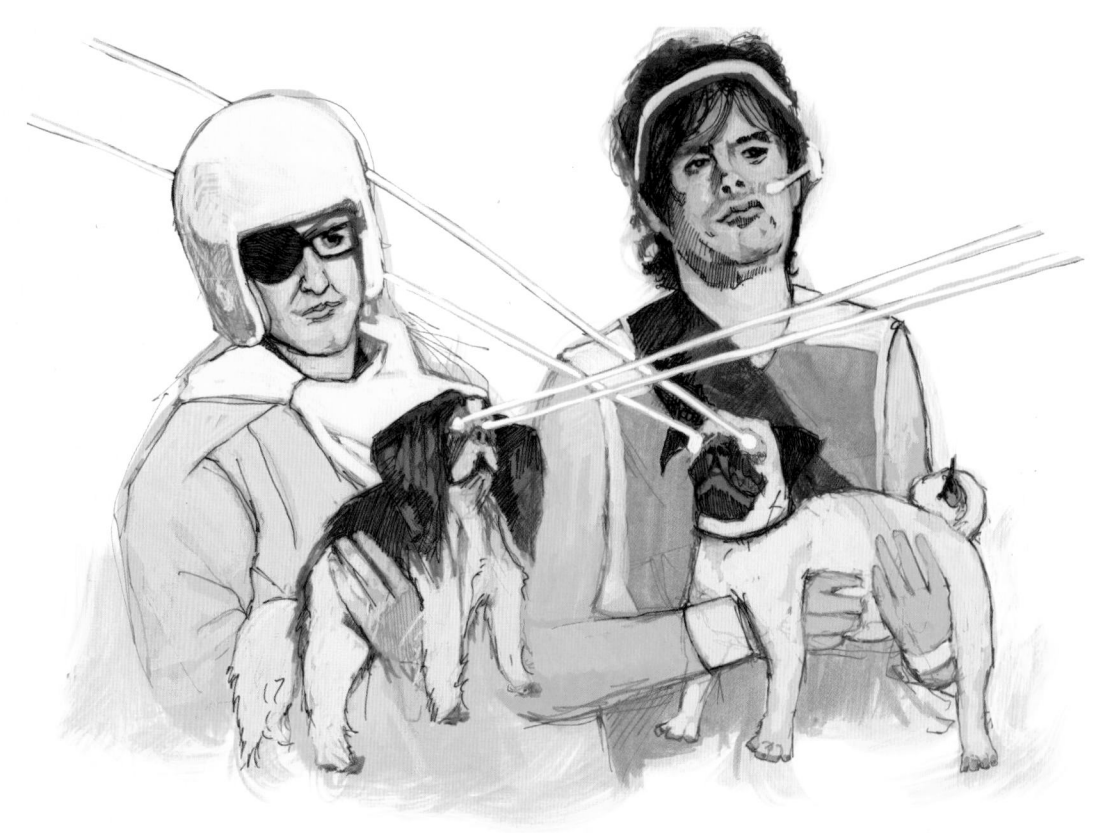

LASER DOGS

LIST YOUR BEST MOVIE-PITCH IDEAS

AKIRA KUROSAWA'S
SEVEN SAMURAI

LIST MOVIES TO SEE SOMEDAY
